Moons of Our Solar System

Kerri O'Donnell

The Rosen Publishing Group's
PowerKids Press™
New York

Published in 2009 by The Rosen Publishing Group, Inc.
29 East 21st Street, New York, NY 10010

Book Design: Daniel Hosek

Photo Credits: Cover © Getty Images; p. 4 © Andrea Danti/Shutterstock; pp. 6 (Earth title), 7, 8 (top), 10 (Mars title), 14 (Jupiter title), 20 (Saturn title), 26 (Neptune title) © Photodisc; p. 8 (bottom) courtesy of Fahad Sulehria (novacelestia.com); pp. 9, 11 (top), 14, 16, 18, 22 (top), 25 (bottom right), 26 (left), 28 (bottom), 29 © Corbis; pp. 10, 11 (bottom), 24 (left), 25 (Cassini), 26 (Uranus title), 30 (bottom) courtesy Wikimedia Commons; p. 12 courtesy NASA Images; pp. 13, 20 courtesy NASA/JPL/Space Science Institute; pp. 15, 26 (right), 27, 28 (top) © NASA/Roger Ressmeyer/Corbis; p. 17 © NASA/epa/Corbis; p. 21 © NASA/JPL/SSI/Handout/CNP/Corbis; pp. 22 (bottom), 25 (bottom left) © epa/Corbis; p. 24 (right) © NASA/JPL/Spac Science Institute/CNP/Corbis; p. 25 (Huygens) © Bettmann/Corbis; p. 30 (Pluto title) © Denis Scott/Corbis.

Library of Congress Cataloging-in-Publication Data

O'Donnell, Kerri, 1972–
 Moons of our solar system / Kerri O'Donnell.
     p. cm.
 Includes index.
 ISBN 978-1-4358-0181-3 (pbk.)
 6-pack ISBN 978-1-4358-0182-0
 ISBN 978-1-4358-2996-1 (lib. bdg.)
 1. Satellites—Juvenile literature. 2. Solar system—Juvenile literature. I. Title.
 QB401.5.O36 2009
 523.9'8-dc22

                                     2009000719

Manufactured in the United States of America

CONTENTS

BEYOND PLANET EARTH

Have you ever looked up at the sky on a clear night and marveled at the countless stars twinkling in the darkness? Did you know that some of those points of light are actually planets?

For thousands of years, people on Earth have gazed up at the night sky wondering what mysteries the heavens held. Ancient astronomers studied the movements of the stars, and ancient peoples created calendars based on what the astronomers saw. Some even thought they could use their observations to learn about future events.

The ancient astronomers noted that brighter heavenly bodies moved among the dimmer stars. They called these bodies "planets" and named them

sun

Mercury

Earth

Venus

Mars

Jupiter

Saturn

Neptune

Uranus

Pluto

res in ancient **mythology**. With the
... of the telescope in the early 1600s,
...ers could see far more than they
...th the naked eye. They could study
...ts in more detail. They eventually
...d that just as Earth has its moon,
the other planets have their own
...n fact, some have many moons!

...is the
...ar to
...ts in
... system.
...the sun,
...uld be
...n Earth.

You may know what the names of the planets are, but do you know whom they were named for?

Mercury—Messenger of the Roman gods

Venus—Roman goddess of love and beauty

Mars—Roman god of war

Jupiter—King of the Roman gods

Saturn—Roman god of agriculture

Uranus—Greek god of the sky

Neptune—Roman god of the sea

Pluto (now considered a dwarf planet)—Roman god of the underworld

A FAMILIAR MOON

Earth's moon is such a familiar sight that you may not think too much about it. But consider this—Earth's moon is just one of 144 known moons, or **satellites**, that orbit the planets in our solar system. Each moon has its own speci[?] qualities. Let's take a look at some of our solar system's magnificent moons!

EARTH'S DOUBLE?

Let's start with our own moon, which is one of the largest in our solar system. With a **diameter** of about 2,155 miles (3,470 km), the moon is about one-third the width of Earth. Some scientists consider Earth and our moon to be a "double planet." Like Earth, the moon spins on its **axis**, but much more slowly than Earth does. It completes one spin each time it orbits Earth. Earth's gravity keeps the moon locked in its orbit, with the same side of the moon facing Earth all the time.

In most ways, the moon is very different from Earth. Earth is covered with vegetation and water, but the moon has no liquid water, no atmosphere, and can't support life. Earth's surface is always changing because of shifts in the plates that make up its crust. The moon doesn't have plates, so its surface only changes when objects from space hit it. The moon is covered with rocky crater[s] huge mountains, and wide canyons.

MAKING THE MOON

Our moon is only about 240,000 miles (386,000 km) from Earth. This might sound far away, but in terms of distances in space, it's very close. It's so

The moon's large, dark areas we see from Earth are called maria, which is a Latin word that means "seas," but they don't contain water. Early astronomers who thought they looked like Earth's seas named them.

Earth's moon
- doesn't have liquid water
- doesn't have life of any kind
- doesn't have an atmosphere
- crust doesn't have plates

- spins on its axis
- has a crust, **mantle**, and core
- has a regular orbit

Earth
- is covered with vegetation, water, and many life-forms
- has an atmosphere
- crust has plates that are always moving

close, in fact, that astronauts have been able to visit, explore, and study the moon in person. As a result, we know much more about the moon than we do about other objects in our solar system. However, no one really knows how the moon was formed.

Scientists have different ideas about how the moon came to be. The most popular one is that a space body about the size of Mars hit Earth (as illustrated below), and the debris from the **collision** came together to form the moon. Scientists think this happened about 4.5 billion years ago, since that's the age of the oldest rock samples collected from the moon.

It's possible that when the moon formed, high temperatures melted the outer layers, and many active volcanoes formed on the moon's surface. These layers then

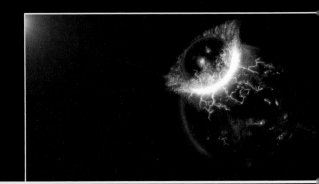

cooled to form the moon's crust. In fact, scientists believe the moon's surface is at least 3 billion years old! If you'd been one of the twelve astronauts who've walked on the moon, you would've seen that it's covered with a thick layer of dust, rock, and boulders.

The six *Apollo* missions were some of the most important space missions the United States has ever conducted. Astronauts from these missions brought back about 840 pounds (380 kg) of moon soil and rock for scientists to study!

THE MOONS OF MARS

Mars

In our solar system, the planets Mercury and Venus are closest to the sun and have no moons at all. The next closest planet to the sun is Earth, which we know has just one moon. Now let's head farther away from the sun to Mars, which we can sometimes see as a red dot in the night sky, and learn a bit about its two moons—Phobos and Deimos (DEE-mohs). Both moons, which were discovered in 1877 by a man named Asaph Hall, may be **asteroids** that were captured by Mars's gravity.

Asaph Hall

PHOBOS

Compared to our moon, Mars's moons are tiny. The larger of the two is Phobos, which was named for one of the sons of Ares, who was the Greek equivalent to Mars, the Roman god of war. Phobos has an uneven rounded shape and measures only about 17 by 14 by 11 miles (27 by 23 by 18 km) in diameter. It orbits Mars twice a day, and its orbit is very close to the planet. Every 100 years, Phobos gets almost 7 feet (2 m) closer to Mars. At that rate, scientists think the moon will crash into Mars in about 50 million years, or it may break up into smaller pieces and form a ring around the planet.

Phobos's surface shows many grooves and craters caused by **meteorites** hitting it. One of the craters, called Stickney, measures about 6 miles (10 km) across. This crater is filled with powdery dust, most likely formed by countless

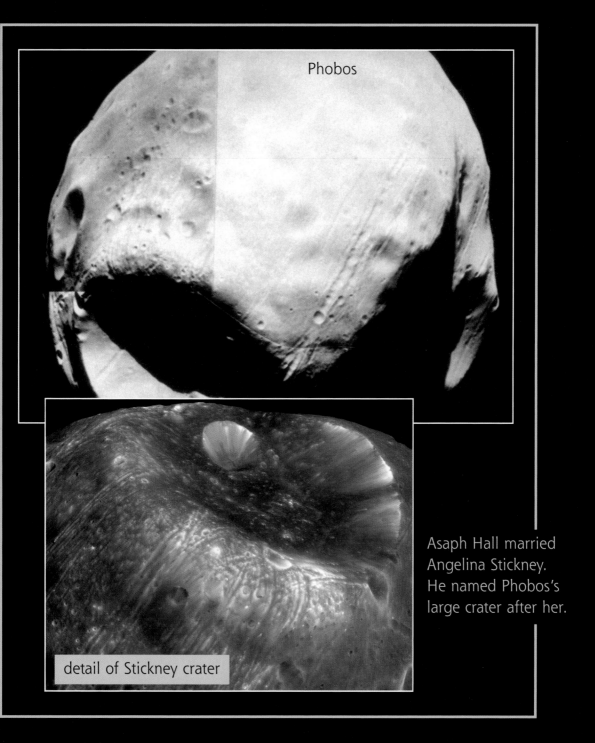

Phobos

detail of Stickney crater

Asaph Hall married
Angelina Stickney.
He named Phobos's
large crater after her.

11

ASTRONAUTS ON MARS'S MOONS?

Did you know scientists have actually talked about using either Phobos or Deimos as a kind of astronaut base? Astronauts could study Mars from these moons and even launch robots to the planet from them!

meteorites hitting the moon's surface over billions of years. The daytime and nighttime temperatures on Phobos are very different. The moon's daytime temperature is around 25°F (–4°C), while its nighttime temperature is around –170°F (–112°C). This large difference likely happens because Phobos has no atmosphere to hold in heat.

DEIMOS

The smaller of Mars's moons is called Deimos, which is the name of the Greek god of fear. Like Phobos, Deimos was the son of Ares, the Greek god of war, and Aphrodite, the Greek goddess of love and beauty. In Greek, the word *deimos* means "terror" or "panic."

Deimos has an irregular shape and looks like a chunk of cratered rock. Deimos is farther from Mars and orbits the planet more slowly than Phobos, completing its orbit once every 30 hours. Deimos's craters are small, and don't appear to be filled with dust as Phobos's are. However, the moon's surface does have a thick layer of loose rocks and dust estimated to be as deep as 330 feet (100 m).

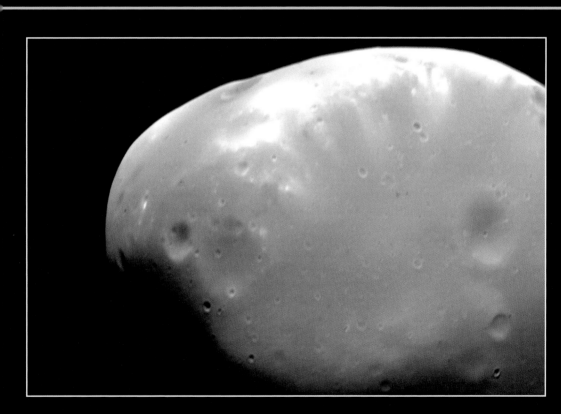

If you were to stand on Deimos, Mars would appear 1,000 times larger and 400 times brighter than a full moon appears to us on Earth!

JUPITER: A MINI-SOLAR SYSTEM!

Jupiter

Beyond Mars is the planet Jupiter, the largest planet in our solar system. Jupiter and its many moons form a kind of mini–solar system. Four of the moons are so large that they're almost like planets orbiting Jupiter, each with its own unique qualities.

THE GALILEAN SATELLITES

In January 1610, an Italian astronomer named Galileo Galilei was looking through a telescope at the night sky when he noticed what he thought were four small stars near Jupiter. What he'd actually discovered were Jupiter's four largest moons. Today, these four moons—Io, Europa, Ganymede, and

Jupiter

Io

Europa

Callisto

Ganymede

Callisto—are known as the Galilean satellites. Around the same time Galileo observed the moons, a German astronomer named Simon Marius may have also observed them. Marius, however, didn't publish his findings, so today Galileo is known as their discoverer.

O: SO MANY VOLCANOES!

Io is the most volcanically active body in our solar system. Its surface, covered by sulfur, has colorful yellow, red, and black splotches. A bit larger than Earth's moon, Io is Jupiter's third largest moon, and the fifth closest to the planet. This moon has such extreme heat within it that much of the layer below its surface is kept in liquid form. This liquid comes up through craters and

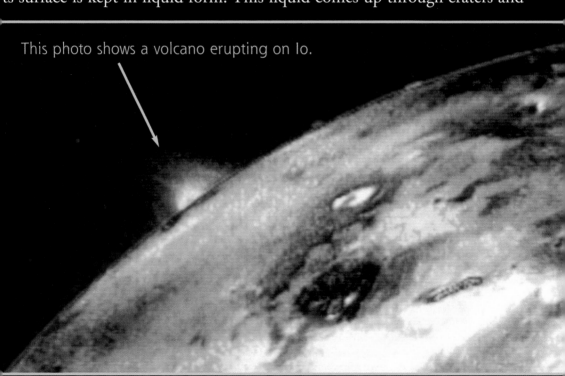

This photo shows a volcano erupting on Io.

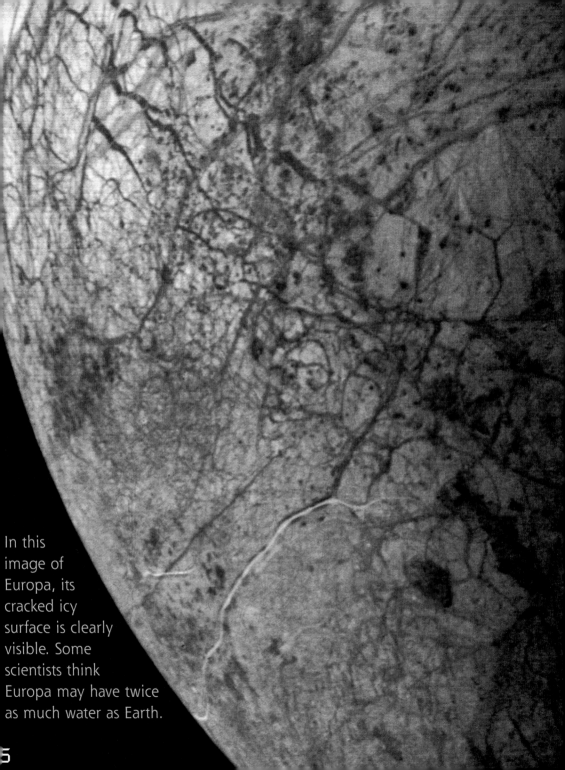

In this image of Europa, its cracked icy surface is clearly visible. Some scientists think Europa may have twice as much water as Earth.

cracks, spreading smooth liquid rock over Io and constantly reforming the moon's surface. Unlike the colder Galilean satellites, Io has no water.

EXPLORING EUROPA

Jupiter's moon Europa is a bit smaller than our moon. It orbits Jupiter about once every 3.5 days. Unlike hot, waterless Io, Europa has plenty of water. Its entire surface is covered by a saltwater ocean. Because it's so far from the sun, the ocean's surface is frozen. Europa's average distance from the sun is about 485,000,000 miles (780,000,000 km), more than five times Earth's distance from the sun. Scientists think Europa's tidal changes actually heat the water below the ocean's icy crust. This means life might exist within Europa's waters!

GANYMEDE: THE LARGEST MOON

With a diameter of about 3,280 miles (5,280 km), Ganymede is not only Jupiter's largest moon, it's the largest moon in our solar system! Scientists think it's made up of rock, metal, water, and ice. Images of Ganymede show craters, mountains, valleys, and what appears to be lava. The brighter spots seen on the moon's surface may have been caused by recent impacts of smaller space objects. A large dark region on the moon's surface, called Galileo Regio,

Galileo Regio

Ganymede is so large that if it were to orbit the sun rather than Jupiter, it would be considered a planet!

17

measures about 2,000 miles (3,200 km) across. Scientists believe that part of this region may be covered with frost.

CALLISTO: A DEAD MOON?

Roughly the size of Mercury, Callisto is the solar system's third largest moon. It's Jupiter's second largest moon, and the Galilean satellite farthest from the planet. Scientists have observed that the moon's surface shows almost no activity

Callisto is the darkest of the Galilean satellites. Scientists think the white spots on its surface are craters filled with ice.

other than changes caused by occasional impacts from space objects. Callisto's surface is one of the most heavily cratered of any object in the solar system.

EVEN MORE MOONS

Of all the planets in our solar system, Jupiter has the most officially named moons, with a current count of sixty-two! Twenty-four were discovered in 2003 alone, so it's possible—and even likely—that more will be found. Jupiter's many smaller outer moons are probably asteroids captured by the planet's gravity.

Below are facts about some of Jupiter's other named moons.

moon	more about it
Metis	• Jupiter's closest moon • diameter measures about 25 miles (40 km) • will someday collide with Jupiter due to changes in its orbit
Amalthea	• Jupiter's fifth largest moon • reddest object in the solar system • last moon to be discovered by visual observation in the night sky (1892)
Himalia	• Jupiter's sixth largest moon • Jupiter's largest irregularly shaped moon
Thebe	• Jupiter's fourth closest moon • surface has large craters and tall mountains

We've already learned about Galileo's discovery of Jupiter's four largest moons in 1610. That same year, he was also the first person to observe Saturn—the sixth planet from the sun—through a telescope. Forty-five years later, a Dutch astronomer named Christiaan Huygens discovered Saturn's first known moon, Titan. To date, fifty-nine more moons have been found, and there are likely more moons yet to be discovered.

Titan

A GIANT MOON

If not for a difference in diameter of just a few miles (km), Saturn's largest moon, Titan, would be the largest moon in the solar system. Titan is larger than both our moon and the planet Mercury, and fascinates scientists because it's the only known moon with an atmosphere more like a planet than a moon. Titan's cloud cover made it difficult at first to photograph its surface features. In 2005, however, a spacecraft was sent beneath the clouds and photographed Titan's surface. It found plains, dunes, mountains, and volcanoes.

Titan is very cold, with a surface temperature of about −290°F (−180°C). Scientists believe its atmosphere, rich in **nitrogen**, may resemble what Earth's atmosphere was like very long ago. The chemicals found in Titan's atmosphere could also mean there may be some kind of life below Titan's clouds!

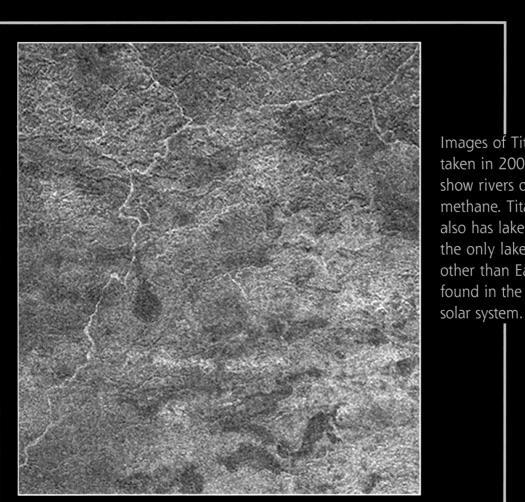

Images of Titan taken in 2006 show rivers of methane. Titan also has lakes—the only lakes other than Earth's found in the solar system.

CASSINI'S DISCOVERIES AND BEYOND

Not long after Huygens discovered Titan, another astronomer, Giovanni Cassini (also known as Jean-Dominique Cassini and Gian Cassini), discovered four more of Saturn's moons—Iapetus, Rhea, Dione, and Tethys. Iapetus has one bright, white **hemisphere** and one that appears completely black. Rhea, which is heavily cratered and icy, is Saturn's second largest moon and the solar system's

Iapetus

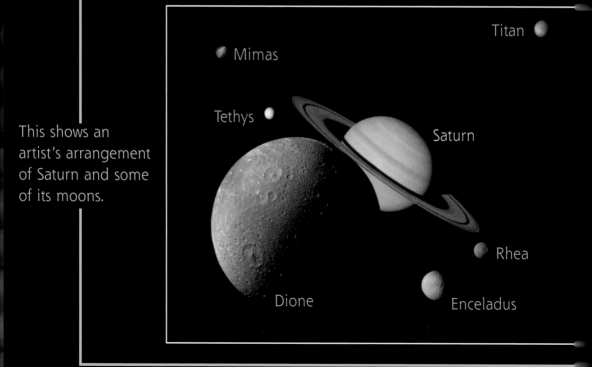

This shows an artist's arrangement of Saturn and some of its moons.

Titan

Mimas

Tethys

Saturn

Dione

Rhea

Enceladus

ninth largest. Its surface features are much like those of Dione, which is also icy and has craters and ice cliffs. Tethys has a **rift** that runs almost three-quarters of the way around it.

Huygens was the first astronomer to describe the ring surrounding Saturn, but it was Cassini who later discovered that the ring is actually several rings. We now know that the rings are mostly made up of water and ice, and that the gravitational force of one of Saturn's moons, Mimas, is the reason for the gap in the rings. Mimas can be identified by its huge crater, which was caused by a force that almost split the moon in two!

Another of Saturn's moons, Enceladus, is slightly larger than Mimas, and is one of the planet's closest moons. It reflects almost all the sunlight it gets and has craters, plains, and icy rifts. A moon called Hyperion

Saturn and Its Moons: Early Discoveries

1610 Galileo Galilei is the first to see Saturn through a telescope.

1655 Christiaan Huygens discovers Saturn's largest moon, Titan.

1659 Huygens writes that a flat ring surrounds Saturn.

1671 Giovanni Cassini discovers Iapetus.

1672 Cassini discovers Rhea.

1675 Cassini first sees a large separation between Saturn's rings.

1684 Cassini discovers Dione and Tethys.

1789 English astronomer William Herschel discovers Mimas and Enceladus.

1848 Hyperion is discovered by American astronomers William Bond and George Bond and English astronomer William Lassell in independent studies.

1898 American astronomer William Henry Pickering discovers Phoebe.

is irregularly shaped and has a surface that resembles a sponge. It rotates without any established pattern, which may mean it recently collided with another space object. Phoebe, the first moon to be discovered through photography, is one of Saturn's outermost moons. It's heavily cratered and orbits Saturn in the opposite direction than Saturn's larger moons orbit.

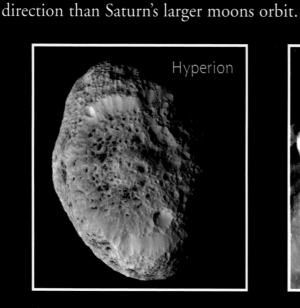
Hyperion

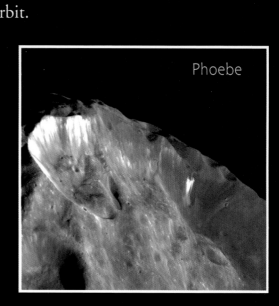
Phoebe

LEARNING MORE ABOUT SATURN AND ITS MOONS

The National **Aeronautics** and Space Administration (NASA) learned much about Saturn and its rings from *Voyager 1* and *Voyager 2*, two spacecraft sent to gather information about the planet in the late 1970s. Today, we're learning even more from the *Cassini-Huygens* spacecraft, which entered the planet's orbit in 2004. The spacecraft has given scientists the most detailed information yet about the planet and its many moons and will continue to do so for several years.

NAME THAT SPACECRAFT!

Giovanni
Cassini

Christi...
Huyge...

The *Cassini-Huygens* spacecraft was named after two astronomers who made many early discoveries about our solar system these men weren't just astronomers. Huygens was also a mathematician and **physicist**, and one of the first people t... propose that light consisted of waves. Like Huygens, Cass... was also a mathematician, as well as an engineer.

NASA and the Europ... Space Agency worke... together to create th... *Cassini-Huygens* space... The left picture is an image of the craft on Saturn. Below shows the craft landing on

THE FARTHEST MOONS

Uranus and Neptune are the farthest planets from the sun. Uranus, the seventh planet from the sun, takes about 84 years to orbit the sun. Neptune, the eighth planet from the sun, takes about 165 years to complete its orbit. We know little about these distant planets, and their moons are just as mysterious.

SHAKESPEARE IN SPACE?

Uranus has twenty-seven discovered moons. While many moons in our solar system are named after figures in Greek and Roman mythology, most of Uranus's moons are named after characters from the works of English authors William Shakespeare and Alexander Pope. Uranus's five largest moons are

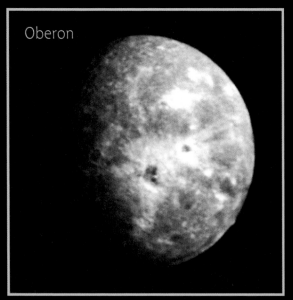

Oberon

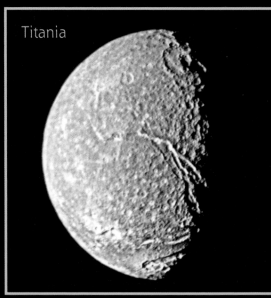

Titania

Oberon, Titania, Umbriel, Ariel, and Miranda. The two largest moons, discovered in 1787 by British astronomer William Herschel, are Oberon and Titania. Titania is the planet's largest moon and the eighth largest in the solar system. Oberon is the most distant of Uranus's five largest moons and has a cratered surface that appears inactive.

Astronomer William Lassell discovered the moons Ariel and Umbriel in 1851. Ariel appears as the brightest of Uranus's moons, and scientists believe it

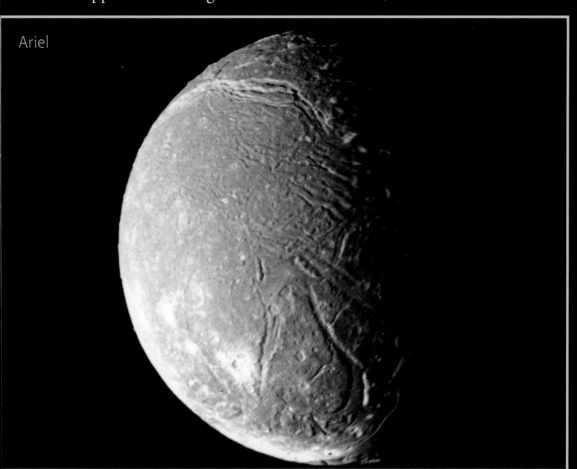

Ariel

also has the youngest surface. Umbriel, the darkest of the five largest moons, is very old. Its cratered surface features a large, bright ring on one side.

Miranda

Miranda, discovered in 1948, is the closest and smallest of Uranus's five largest moons. It is also perhaps the oddest-looking, with canyons that are more than 10 times deeper than the Grand Canyon! Beyond Miranda, eight small moons orbit Uranus very close together; so close that scientists don't know why they haven't collided with each other!

TRITON'S DEEP FREEZE

Of Neptune's thirteen known moons, the largest is Triton. It was discovered in 1846, just 17 days after Neptune itself had been discovered. Triton's ice-covered surface reflects most of the sunlight that hits it, making it

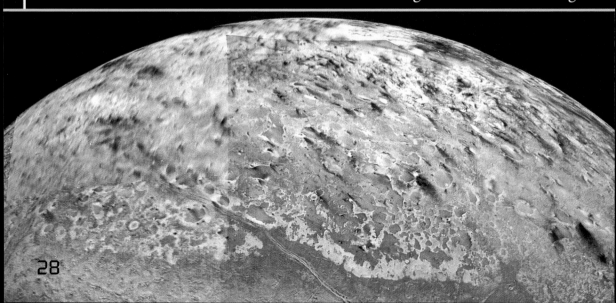

painting of *Voyager 2*

he coldest known body in
our solar system with a
surface temperature of about
-400°F (-240°C). **Geysers** on
Triton's surface shoot an icy
mixture more than 5 miles (8
km) up into the thin
atmosphere, where it freezes
and falls as snow. We know this from data gathered by NASA's *Voyager 2* in
1989. Scientists have also learned that Triton's atmosphere is getting warmer,
although the reason for this is unclear.

DARK MOONS

Until recently, only two of Neptune's moons—Triton and Nereid—were
known. Nereid was discovered in 1949. *Voyager 2*'s mission not only gathered
important information about Triton—it also discovered six more dark moons
that had previously been undetected. In 2002 and 2003, astronomers discovered
another five moons, and may find even more in the future.

Triton is so huge that it makes up more than
99% of the total mass that orbits Neptune.

A DWARF PLANET AND ITS MOONS

Pluto

Discovered in 1930, Pluto was once considered the farthest planet from the sun in our solar system. In 2006, it was renamed as a "dwarf planet" because it lacks certain traits shared by the other planets. Even though it's no longer called a planet, Pluto does have moons that orbit it.

The largest moon, Charon, was discovered in 1978. It's about half the size of Pluto, but does not orbit it. Some scientists think Pluto and Charon should be called a double planet! Charon's surface seems to be covered with frozen water, possibly made from material Pluto lost when it collided with another space body. Two other known moons, Hydra and Nix, were discovered in 2005. In 2006, NASA sent the *New Horizons* spacecraft to explore Pluto and its moons. Perhaps it will find there are even more moons in our solar system!

This picture shows an artist's idea of the surface of Pluto's moon, Hydra. Pluto and Charon are shown in the background, and Nix appears as the bright dot to the left.

Charon

Pluto

Nix

GLOSSARY

aeronautics (ehr-uh-NAW-tiks) The science of the design and operation of aircraft and spacecraft.

asteroid (AS-tuh-roid) A rock-like object found in space that orbits the sun.

axis (AK-suhs) An imaginary line around which an object turns.

collision (kuh-LIH-zhun) A crash.

diameter (dy-AA-muh-tuhr) A straight line passing from one side of a circle or sphere through the center to the other side.

geyser (GY-zuhr) A spring that sends up fountains or jets of hot water or steam.

hemisphere (HEH-muh-sfihr) A half of a sphere or globe.

mantle (MAN-tuhl) The layer between the core and the crust of a planet or moon.

meteorite (MEE-tee-uh-ryt) A mass of stone or metal.

mythology (mih-THAH-luh-jee) A collection of myths or stories.

nitrogen (NY-truh-juhn) A colorless, tasteless, odorless gas which makes up much of the air.

physicist (FIH-zuh-sihst) Someone who studies matter and energy.

rift (RIFT) A break in the crust of a planet or moon.

satellite (SA-tuh-lyt) An object that circles a planet.

INDEX

Due to the changing nature of Internet links, The Rosen Publishing Group, Inc., has developed an online list of Web sites related to the subject of this book. This site is updated regularly. Please use this link to access the list: http://www.rcbmlinks.com/rlr/moons